Photography by Mike Cooper and Günter Beer.
Additional photos used under license from Shutterstock.com.

ISBN 978-1-64638-879-0

Printed in China

Love Food™ is an imprint of Cottage Door Press, LLC.
Parragon® and the Parragon® logo are registered
trademarks of Cottage Door Press, LLC.

Notes for the Reader

This book uses standard kitchen measuring spoons and cups.
All spoon and cup measurements are level unless otherwise
indicated. Unless otherwise stated, milk is assumed to be
whole, eggs are large, individual vegetables are medium, and
pepper is freshly ground black pepper. Unless otherwise stated,
all root vegetables should be peeled prior to using. People
with nut allergies should be aware that some of the prepared
ingredients used in the recipes in this book may contain nuts.

Garnishes, decorations, and serving suggestions are all optional and
not necessarily included in the recipe ingredients or method. The
times given are only an approximate guide. Preparation times differ
according to the techniques used by different people and the cooking
times may also vary from those given. Optional ingredients, variations,
or serving suggestions have not been included in the time calculations.

Please consume alcohol responsibly.

THE ART OF MIXOLOGY

MAKING SPIRITS BRIGHT

PaRragon.

CONTENTS

INTRODUCTION

There's no denying it: Christmas is truly a magical time of year. There's the crisp bite of winter air, the smell of pine needles, twinkling lights, and, if you're lucky, a few jingle bells jingling, too. And that's just outside. Inside cozy homes everywhere, the smell of freshly baked cookies mingles with the scent of a real Christmas tree. Good food roasting in the oven draws generations of family and friends to the table to gather together.

And there's no denying that a good cocktail is the perfect compliment to a day of decorating the house or freshly cut tree or to a good meal among loved ones. In this book, you'll find a collection of Christmas cocktails perfect for any occasion or festive activity.

You can enjoy decorating the Christmas tree with a Cinnamon Basil Mojito (page 39) or The Poinsettia (page 40) in hand, or warm up after spending a day out in the cold with a Hot Brandy Chocolate (page 61) or a glass of Mulled Wine (page 73). And hosting a joyful Christmas party or Christmas brunch will go off without a hitch if you're serving a bowl of Holiday Eggnog (page 85) or a Champagne Pick-Me-Up (page 90).

It's also worth noting that any of the recipes included here can easily be made as a mocktail for children or for adults who prefer their drinks sans alcohol. These drinks are sure to make everyone's spirits very bright indeed.

GLASSWARE

Presentation is everything in mixology, so it is important to serve a cocktail in the appropriate glass—the size, shape, and style all have an impact on the visual perception and enjoyment of the drink. Here are some of the classic glasses you will need to have in your collection.

Martini Glass
The most iconic of all cocktail glasses, the conical glass emerged with the art deco movement. The long stem is perfect for chilled drinks, because it keeps people's hands from inadvertently warming the cocktail.

Highball Glass
Sometimes known as a Collins glass, these glasses are perfect for serving drinks with a high proportion of mixer to alcohol. The highball glass is versatile enough to be a substitute for the similarly shaped, but slightly larger, Collins glass.

Old-Fashioned Glass
The lowball glass, also known as a rocks glass, is a short, squat tumbler and is great for serving any alcohol on the rocks, or for short, mixed cocktails.

Champagne Flute
The tall, thin flute's tapered design reduces the champagne's surface area and so helps to keep the fizz in the drink for longer. The flute has now largely replaced the coupe glass for serving champagne and champagne cocktails.

SHOT GLASS

This glass is a home bar essential and can hold just enough alcohol to be drunk in one mouthful. It also has a firm base that can be satisfyingly slammed on a bar top. The shot glass can also stand in for a measure when making cocktails.

MARGARITA GLASS

The margarita, or coupette, glass, as its name implies, was designed specifically for serving margaritas. It is ideal for any frozen, blended drinks.

COUPE GLASS

A wide-rim glass that is good for serving sparkling drinks was once the glass of choice for champagne. Legend has it that the glass was inspired by the shape of a woman's breast.

SNIFTER GLASS

The bowl-shape snifter glass invites drinkers to cradle the drink in their hands, warming the contents of the glass—it is good for winter liquors, such as brandy. The aroma of the drink is held in the glass, allowing you to breathe in the drink before sipping.

HURRICANE GLASS

This pear-shaped glass pays homage to the hurricane lamp and was used to create the New Orleans rum-based cocktail: the Hurricane. It's also used for a variety of frozen and blended cocktails.

ICED BEVERAGE GLASS

A variation on the highball glass that combines a tapered, tall bowl with a short stem, this glass is ideal for serving chilled drinks.

IRISH COFFEE GLASS

The mug of this type of glass typically sits on top of a decorative pedestal foot. Its handle makes it an elegant and safe way to enjoy hot beverages.

MIXOLOGY EQUIPMENT

The equipment you have in your home bar depends on whether you are a cocktail king or queen who likes all the latest gadgets, or whether you are prepared to make do with some basic options. Nowadays, there is no limit to the amount of bar equipment available, but you definitely won't need a lot of gimmicky gadgets to make the majority of the drinks in this book. Here is an outline of the essential tools of the trade.

JIGGERS

A jigger is a bartender's basic measuring tool and is essential for crafting the perfect blend of ingredients. It usually has a measurement on each end, such as 1 ounce and 1½ ounces. Look for a steel jigger with clear measurement markings so you can easily and accurately pour out the measures.

BARSPOON

A proper barspoon has a small bowl and a long handle that allows you to muddle, mix, and stir with ease. Spoons come in a variety of lengths and widths, and a stylish barspoon is an attractive addition to any bartender's equipment.

SHAKER

Most contemporary shakers are made from steel, because steel doesn't tarnish readily and doesn't conduct heat easily—this is useful for chilled cocktails, because the ice cools the cocktail instead of the shaker. Most standard shakers come with a built-in strainer, but if you're using a Boston or Parisian shaker, you'll need to use a separate strainer.

MIXING GLASS

Any vessel that holds about 2 cups of liquid can be used for mixing drinks. It is good to have a mixing glass with a spout or ridged rim so that you can stop ice from slipping into the glass; however, this is not vital, because you can always use a strainer. Mixing glasses are increasingly popular, and they are usually made of glass or crystal.

MUDDLER

For mashing up citrus fruit or crushing herbs, you need a muddler. This is a chunky wooden tool with a rounded end, and it can also be used to make cracked ice. You can mash fruit or crush herbs with a mortar and pestle, but the advantage of a muddler is that it can be used directly in the mixing glass.

STRAINER

A bar or Hawthorne strainer is an essential tool to prevent ice and other ingredients from being poured into your glass. Some cocktails need to be double strained, so even if there is a strainer in your cocktail shaker, you'll still need a separate Hawthorne strainer in your bar collection.

JUICER

A traditional juicer, with a ridged half-lemon shape on a saucer, works well for juicing small amounts. There is also a citrus spout available that screws into a lemon or lime; it is useful for obtaining tiny amounts of juice. Mechanical or electric presses are great for large amounts of juice, but they are not essential in a home bar.

OTHER EQUIPMENT

Other items you might need in your home bar equipment are a corkscrew, bottle opener, decorative toothpicks, blender, tongs, ice bucket, cutting board, knives, pitchers, swizzle sticks, straws, and an espuma gun for making foams.

MIXOLOGY TECHNIQUES

SHAKING AND STIRRING

These are the two most basic mixology techniques, and they are essential to master to confidently make a range of classic and craft cocktails. Shaking is when you add all the ingredients, with the specified amount of ice cubes, to the shaker and shake vigorously for 5–10 seconds. The benefits of shaking are that the drink is rapidly mixed, chilled, and aerated. Once the drink has been shaken, the outside of the shaker should be lightly frosted. Shaking a cocktail will dilute your drink significantly. This is an essential part of the cocktail-making process and gives recipes the correct balance of taste, strength, and temperature. After shaking, the drink is double strained into glasses—the shaker should have a built-in strainer, but you may also use a separate strainer over the glass. Shaking can also be used to prepare cocktails that include an ingredient that will not combine with less vigorous forms of mixing, such as an egg white.

Stirring is the purist's choice. This is a mixing technique where you add all the ingredients, usually with some ice cubes, but you combine them in a mixing glass and then stir the ingredients together using a long-handled barspoon or swizzle stick. This allows for you to blend and chill the ingredients without too much erosion of the ice, so you can control the level of dilution and keep it to a minimum.

BUILDING AND LAYERING

Building is a technique of pouring all the ingredients, one by one, usually over ice into the serving glass. You might then stir the cocktail briefly, but this is just to mix instead of to chill or aerate. The order the ingredients are added can change from drink to drink, which can affect the final flavor.

Another important bartending skill is the art of layering, requiring concentration, precision, and a steady hand. To make layered drinks, you generally pour the heaviest liquid first, working to the lightest. The real trick is the technique. Touch the top of the drink with a long-handled barspoon and pour the liquid slowly over the back of it to disperse it across the top of the ingredients already in the glass. Be sure to use a clean barspoon for each layer. Floating is the term used to describe adding the top layer.

MUDDLING AND BLENDING

Muddling is the extraction of the juice or oils from the pulp or skin of a fruit, herb, or spice and involves mashing ingredients to release their flavors. It's usually done with a wooden pestle-like implement called a muddler. (If you don't have a muddler, use a mortar and pestle or the end of a wooden spoon.) The best muddling technique is to keep pressing down with a twisting action until the ingredient has released all its oil or juice.

Blending is when all the cocktail ingredients are combined in a blender or food processor. This technique is often used when mixing alcohol with fruit or with creamy ingredients that do not combine well otherwise. Use crushed or cracked ice to produce cocktails with a smooth, frozen consistency.

FOAMS

Foams and airs can be created in various thicknesses, from a light froth to a heavy, creamy foam. For a simple foam, use egg white, lemon juice, and sugar. To top two cocktails, whisk 1 egg white with ½ ounce of lemon juice and 1 teaspoon of granulated sugar until thoroughly mixed. Put the mixture into an espuma gun or cream whipper, then charge, shake, and spray it over the top of the cocktails for a light, creamy finish. The fresher the egg white, the more stable the foam, so use fresh eggs.

CHAPTER ONE

IT'S BEGINNING TO LOOK A LOT LIKE CHRISTMAS

It's beginning to look a lot like Christmas...and in this section you'll see recognizable, classic cocktails that feature seasonal flavors for a festive twist. With one of these in hand, you'll be in the Christmas spirit in no time.

MISTLETOE MARTINI

SERVES 1

1½ ounces vodka
½ ounce elderflower
    liqueur
1½ ounces cranberry juice
½ ounce simple syrup
cranberries, to garnish
rosemary sprig, to garnish

1. Fill a cocktail shaker with ice,
   then add the vodka, elderflower
   liqueur, cranberry juice, and
   simple syrup. Shake until chilled.

2. Strain into a martini glass.
   Garnish by floating a
   few cranberries and
   rosemary sprig on top.

HOLIDAY NEGRONI

SERVES 8

8 ounces spice-infused
    Campari
8 ounces gin
8 ounces sweet vermouth

SPICE-INFUSED CAMPARI
8 ounces Campari
2 oranges, divided
4 star anise pods, plus
    more for serving
3 cinnamon sticks, plus
    more to garnish
2 teaspoons pink
    peppercorns, crushed
1 teaspoon whole cloves

1. Pour Campari into a 1-cup
   lidded jar, then add zest
   from half of one orange.

2. Toast the star anise, cinnamon,
   peppercorns, and cloves in a
   small saucepan over medium-low
   heat, stirring frequently, until
   fragrant, 3 to 4 minutes. Add
   spices to the jar with the Campari
   and zest. Seal, shake, and let sit
   at room temperature overnight.
   The next day, strain the liquid
   and discard the solids.

3. Fill each glass with ice, then mix
   in 1 ounce of infused Campari,
   1 ounce of gin, and 1 ounce
   of sweet vermouth. Garnish
   with orange zest, star anise,
   and cinnamon sticks.

APPLE CINNAMON OLD FASHIONED

SERVES 1

1 tablespoon apple butter
2 ounces bourbon
6 dashes bitters
club soda
cinnamon stick,
    to garnish
apple slice, to garnish

1. Combine apple butter, bourbon, and bitters in a cocktail shaker and shake well.

2. Pour into glass and top with club soda. Garnish with cinnamon stick and an apple slice.

MERRY MAI TAI

SERVES 1

2 ounces pineapple juice
2 ounces blood orange
    juice
1 ounce dark rum
1 ounce amaretto
cranberries, to garnish
sprig of mint, to garnish
orange slice, to garnish

1. Fill a cocktail shaker with crushed ice, juices, rum, and amaretto, and shake lightly.

2. Strain into a glass full of ice. Garnish with cranberries, an orange slice, and sprig of mint.

CRANBERRY MULE

SERVES 1

2 tablespoons
    cranberry syrup
1¾ ounces white rum
3½ ounces ginger beer
frozen cranberries,
    to garnish

CRANBERRY SYRUP
1 cup frozen cranberries
½ cup granulated sugar
1 cup water

1. First make the cranberry syrup by adding the cranberries, sugar, and water to a small saucepan. Cook over low heat, stirring occasionally, until the sugar has completely dissolved, then increase the heat slightly and simmer for about 5 minutes or until the cranberries have burst and the liquid is thick and syrupy. Cover and leave to cool.

2. Puree if desired, then pour into a sterilized, sealable jar and chill in the refrigerator.

3. To make the cocktail, add 2 tablespoons of the cranberry syrup to a glass filled with ice. The rest of the syrup can be stored in the refrigerator for up to 3 days.

4. Add the white rum and ginger beer to a cocktail shaker with some ice. Shake together until well frosted and frothy. Slowly pour into the glass to create a two-tone effect. Garnish with a few frozen cranberries.

EGGNOG WHITE RUSSIAN

SERVES 2

3½ ounces vodka
3½ ounces coffee liqueur
3 ounces eggnog
½ teaspoon sea salt
ground nutmeg,
    to garnish

1. Stir the vodka, coffee liqueur,
   and eggnog in a mixing glass
   with ice until well chilled.
   Pour into two glasses.

2. Once combined, sprinkle
   each with some of the salt and
   ground nutmeg to garnish.

GINGER WHISKY MAC

SERVES 1

1¾ ounces Scotch whisky
¾ ounce ginger wine

1. Pour the Scotch whisky into an old-fashioned glass.

2. Add the ginger wine. Add a few ice cubes and lightly stir.

CRANBERRY COLLINS

SERVES 1

1¾ ounces vodka
¾ ounce elderflower
   syrup
2½ ounces cranberry juice
club soda
lime slice and lime peel
   twist, to garnish

1. Put ice into a cocktail shaker.

2. Pour the vodka, elderflower syrup, and cranberry juice over the ice and shake until well frosted.

3. Strain into a collins or highball glass filled with ice. Top up with club soda and garnish with the lime slice and peel.

APPLE BRANDY SOUR

SERVES 1

1¾ ounces apple brandy
¾ ounce lemon juice
½ ounce simple syrup
lemon slice, to garnish

1. Put ice cubes into a cocktail shaker.

2. Pour the apple brandy, lemon juice, and simple syrup over the ice, then shake thoroughly until well frosted.

3. Fill an old-fashioned glass with ice cubes. Strain the cocktail into the glass. Garnish the glass with the lemon slice.

WINTER DAIQUIRI

SERVES 1

spice-infused golden rum
2 teaspoons fresh
    orange juice
2 teaspoons fresh
    lime juice
1 teaspoon water
1 teaspoon granulated
    sugar
large pinch ground
    cinnamon

SPICE-INFUSED
GOLDEN RUM
1¾ ounces golden rum
2 teaspoons honey
2 strips orange zest
1-inch piece cinnamon
    stick, halved
1 thin slice fresh ginger
1 allspice berry, crushed

1. To make spice-infused golden rum, add the rum, honey, orange strips, cinnamon, ginger, and allspice to a small saucepan and warm gently together for 1–2 minutes. Remove from the heat and leave to cool for at least 1 hour, or longer if you have time, so that the flavors can infuse together.

2. When ready to serve, strain the infused rum into a cocktail shaker, reserving the aromatics. Add the orange and lime juices and ice, then shake together gently until well frosted.

3. To "frost" the glass, add the water to a saucer. Add the sugar and ground cinnamon to a second saucer. Dip the rim of a cocktail glass first in the water, then in the sugar. Cut some of the reserved orange into thin strips and add to the glass with a long, thin sliver of the reserved cinnamon. Strain the daiquiri into the glass.

CHAPTER TWO

DECK THE HALLS

*Here you'll find just the right cocktail to sip while hanging garlands,
ornaments, and maybe even boughs of holly. These recipes feature
botanical notes that infuse each cocktail with aromatic flavors.*

CINNAMON BASIL MOJITO

SERVES 1

6–8 cinnamon basil leaves
1½ ounces spiced rum
1 ounce pomegranate juice
½ lime, juiced
1 ounce simple syrup
dash of ground cinnamon
club soda
sprig of cinnamon
    basil, to garnish
pomegranate seeds,
    to garnish
lime twist, to garnish

1. In a cocktail shaker, muddle the first six ingredients together.

2. Strain mixture over an ice-filled cocktail glass and top with club soda. Garnish with a fresh sprig of cinnamon basil, pomegranate seeds, and lime twist.

THE POINSETTIA

SERVES 2

4 ounces pure
    cranberry juice
8 ounces sparkling wine
cranberries, to garnish
rosemary sprig, to garnish

1. Pour 2 ounces of cranberry juice in each champagne glass. Fill the rest of the glass with sparkling wine.

2. Garnish with a few cranberries and rosemary sprig.

CHRISTMAS GIN COCKTAIL

SERVES 2

2 ounces pomegranate
    juice
2 ounces fresh
    orange juice
2 teaspoons honey
16 ounces sparkling water
4 ounces gin
pomegranate seeds,
    to garnish

1. Add pomegranate juice, orange juice, honey, sparkling water, and gin to a cocktail shaker. Lightly shake until all ingredients are combined.

2. Strain over ice-filled cocktail glasses. Garnish with pomegranate seeds.

CRANBERRY KRINGLE

SERVES 1

3 ounces cranberry
   juice cocktail
1 ounce peach schnapps
1 ounce vodka
cranberries, to garnish
sprig of fresh mint,
   to garnish

1. Place the first three ingredients in a cocktail shaker and shake well to combine.

2. Pour into a glass filled with ice. Garnish with cranberries and fresh mint.

POM POM

SERVES 1

juice of ½ lemon
1 egg white
1 dash grenadine
lemon-lime soda
lemon slice, to garnish

1. Shake the lemon juice, egg white, and grenadine together and strain into a chilled coupe glass.

2. Top with lemon-lime soda and garnish with a lemon slice on the rim of the glass.

APPLE CLASSIC

SERVES 1

½ ounce gin
½ ounce brandy
½ ounce Calvados or
    other apple brandy
sweet hard cider
apple slice, to garnish

1. Shake the gin, brandy, and Calvados over ice until frosted.

2. Strain into a glass and top with hard cider to taste. Garnish with a slice of apple.

GINGER GARLAND

SERVES 1

1¾ ounces golden rum
¾ ounce whiskey liqueur
¾ ounce ginger syrup
club soda

1. Shake the golden rum, whiskey liqueur, and ginger syrup over ice until well frosted.

2. Pour into a chilled cocktail glass filled with ice. Top with club soda to taste.

ORANGE GIN SLING

SERVES 1

1 sugar cube
¾ ounce gin
4 dashes of orange bitters
freshly grated nutmeg,
    to garnish

1. Place the sugar in an old-fashioned glass and add 4 ounces of hot water. Stir until the sugar is dissolved.

2. Stir in the gin and orange bitters, then sprinkle with nutmeg.

THE CHRISTMAS ROSE

SERVES 1

1¾ ounces gin
6 ounces cranberry juice
1 tablespoon honey
¼ teaspoon rose water
1 tablespoon
   pomegranate seeds
¼ teaspoon dried
   rose petals, plus
   extra to garnish

1. Pour the gin, cranberry juice, honey, and rose water into a Collins or highball glass.

2. Stir with a barspoon until the honey has dissolved.

3. Add a few ice cubes, the pomegranate seeds, and rose petals, then stir again.

4. Garnish with the rose petals and serve with a straw.

CHAPTER THREE

Whether you've been playing in the snow with little ones or cutting down the most perfect Christmas tree, the drinks in this section offer a hint of brandy or rum to help warm you up after being outside on a cold winter's day.

HOT CARAMEL LATTE

SERVES 2

1¾ ounces alcohol of
   choice (bourbon, rum,
   Irish cream liqueur,
   coffee liqueur, etc.)
¼ cup granulated sugar
⅓ cup water
1¼ cups milk
½ cup hot espresso

VARIATION

*For a festive winter latte,
substitute 2 tablespoons
of gingerbread-flavored
syrup for the caramel.
Omit steps 1, 2, and 4.*

1. To make the caramel, put the sugar and 2 tablespoons of the water into a small, heavy saucepan. Heat gently until the sugar dissolves, then boil rapidly for 4–5 minutes, without stirring, until the mixture turns to a golden caramel.

2. Remove from the heat and carefully pour in the remaining water. Stir until the caramel dissolves, then return the pan to the heat and simmer for an additional 3–4 minutes, until syrupy.

3. Put the milk into a separate saucepan and heat over medium heat until almost boiling. Remove from the heat, pour in the espresso and almost all the caramel sauce, and whisk until frothy. Divide between two tall latte glasses.

4. Drizzle the remaining caramel sauce over the top.

BRANDY HOT CHOCOLATE

SERVES 4

4 cups milk
4 ounces semisweet
    chocolate, chopped
2 tablespoons sugar
3 ounces brandy
½ cup whipped cream
freshly grated nutmeg or
    unsweetened cocoa
    powder, for sprinkling

1. Heat the milk in a small
   saucepan until almost boiling.

2. Add the chocolate and sugar
   and stir over low heat until
   the chocolate has melted.

3. Pour into four warm heatproof
   glasses, then pour ¾ ounce
   of the brandy over the back
   of a spoon on top of each.

4. Top with the whipped cream and
   sprinkle with the grated nutmeg.

HOT BUTTERED RUM

SERVES 1

¾ ounce dark rum
1 teaspoon packed dark
   brown sugar
5 ounces hot water
1 teaspoon salted butter
¼ teaspoon allspice

1. In an old-fashioned glass, mix together the rum, brown sugar, and hot water with a teaspoon until the sugar has completely dissolved.

2. Place the butter on top. Sprinkle with the allspice.

3. Serve when the butter has melted.

SALTED CARAMEL RUM HOT COCOA

SERVES 4

2 tablespoons
    granulated sugar
1 tablespoon water
salt flakes
7 ounces milk
1½ ounces semisweet
    chocolate, broken
    into pieces
1 teaspoon unsweetened
    cocoa powder
pinch ground cinnamon
¾ ounce dark rum
shaved or grated
    semisweet chocolate,
    to garnish
mini marshmallows,
    to serve

1. Add the sugar and water to a small heavy saucepan and heat gently, without stirring, until the sugar has completely dissolved.

2. Bring to a boil and boil rapidly for 4–5 minutes, without stirring, until the simple syrup begins to turn golden around the edges. Keep a very close eye on it at this stage and continue to heat until the syrup is a rich golden brown all over.

3. Remove the pan from the heat, add the salt, swirl to mix, then gradually pour in the milk. Stand back while you add the milk as the syrup can splatter. Put the pan back over low heat and stir to mix the caramel and milk together. Add the chocolate. Stir the cocoa powder with a little water to make a paste and add it with the cinnamon. Keep stirring until smooth.

4. When the chocolate mix is hot but not boiling, stir in the rum, warm together, then pour into four heatproof glass mugs. Sprinkle with shaved or grated chocolate. Add mini marshmallows, if desired.

HOT TODDY

SERVES 1

6 ounces water
1½ ounces whiskey
2–3 teaspoons
   honey, to taste
2–3 teaspoons lemon
   juice, to taste
1 lemon slice, to garnish
cinnamon stick,
   to garnish
star anise, to garnish

1. In a saucepan, bring the water to a simmer. Once hot, pour into a mug.

2. Add the whiskey, 2 teaspoons honey and 2 teaspoons lemon juice. Stir until the honey has disappeared into the hot water. Taste, and add 1 teaspoon honey for more sweetness, and/or 1 teaspoon more lemon juice for more zing.

3. Garnish with a lemon slice, cinnamon stick, and star anise.

BOURBON APPLE CIDER

SERVES 10

½ gallon apple cider
2–3 cups bourbon
1 apple, sliced, reserve
    some to garnish
1 pear, sliced, reserve
    some to garnish
16 cinnamon sticks
10 fresh rosemary
    sprigs, to garnish

1. In a large pot, combine apple cider, bourbon, apple and pear slices, and 6 cinnamon sticks, and heat on medium-low for 10 minutes.

2. Reduce to low heat to keep warm. Garnish with reserved apple slices, cinnamon sticks, and a sprig of fresh rosemary, and serve warm.

MULLED ALE

SERVES 5

4½ pints strong ale
10 ounces brandy
2 tablespoons
    granulated sugar
large pinch of
    ground cloves
large pinch of
    ground ginger

1. Put all ingredients in a heavy-bottomed saucepan and heat gently, stirring until the sugar has dissolved. Continue to heat so that it is simmering but not boiling.

2. Remove the saucepan from the heat and serve the ale immediately in a heatproof glass.

MULLED WINE

SERVES 4

3 cups red wine
1¾ ounces sherry
8 cloves
1 cinnamon stick
½ teaspoon ground
    allspice
2 tablespoons honey
1 orange, cut into wedges
1 lemon, cut into wedges

1. Put the wine, sherry, cloves, cinnamon, allspice, and honey into a pan. Warm over low heat, stirring, until just starting to simmer, but do not let it boil.

2. Remove from the heat and pour through a strainer. Discard the cloves and cinnamon stick.

3. Return the pan to the heat with the orange and lemon wedges and warm gently. Pour into 4 warmed heatproof glasses.

RUM NOGGIN

SERVES 8

6 eggs
4–5 teaspoons
confectioner's sugar
freshly grated nutmeg,
plus extra for
sprinkling
16 ounces (2 cups)
dark rum
5 cups milk, warmed

1. Whisk the eggs in a punch bowl with the sugar and a little nutmeg.

2. Whisk in the rum and gradually stir in the milk.

3. Warm through gently, if desired, and serve in heatproof glasses or mugs, sprinkled with nutmeg.

CHRISTMAS COW

SERVES 1

1 cup milk
1¾ ounces Irish whiskey
1 teaspoon confectioner's
    sugar

1. Heat the milk in a small saucepan just until the milk starts to boil.

2. Remove from the heat and pour into a warmed punch glass.

3. Pour in the whiskey and sugar and stir until the sugar has dissolved.

CHAPTER FOUR

ROCKIN' AROUND THE CHRISTMAS TREE

The guests have arrived and it's time to celebrate! This chapter provides a truly fun collection of punches and fizzy cocktails ready for sharing—all perfect for a festive party.

CHRISTMAS PUNCH

SERVES 20

40 ounces pure
    cranberry juice
2 bottles (750 ml each)
    dry sparkling wine,
    like champagne,
    cava, or prosecco
16 ounces apple cider
12 ounces ginger ale
12 ounces dark rum
    or brandy
2 oranges, thinly sliced
    into rounds
1 cup fresh cranberries
handful of star anise
sprigs of fresh rosemary

1. Fill a large punch bowl with ice, then add the chilled cranberry juice, sparkling wine, apple cider, ginger ale, and rum. Stir gently to combine.

2. Top with the orange slices, fresh cranberries, star anise, and rosemary sprigs.

JINGLE JUICE PUNCH

SERVES 16

1 bottle (750ml) whipped
cream flavored vodka
1 bottle pink champagne
or sparkling rosé
1 (2 liter) bottle cherry
flavored lemon
lime soda
cranberries, to garnish

1. Fill a large punch bowl with
ice, then add the first three
ingredients and stir well.

2. Garnish with floating cranberries.

HOLIDAY EGGNOG

SERVES 9

6 large eggs
7 tablespoons
    granulated sugar, plus
    2 tablespoons extra
18 ounces heavy cream
18 ounces milk
4 ounces brandy
2 ounces light rum
1 teaspoon vanilla extract
18 ounces whipping cream
freshly grated nutmeg,
    to garnish

1. Whisk the eggs on medium speed until thick and lemon in color, then gradually add 7 tablespoons of sugar until combined.

2. Put the heavy cream and milk into a large saucepan over a medium-low heat and hear until very hot but not boiling. Gradually add the hot milk mixture to the egg mixture, stirring with a whisk. Return the mixture to the pan and cook over a medium-low heat, stirring constantly until very hot but not boiling. Remove from the heat and leave to cool. Stir in the brandy, rum, and vanilla extract. Cover and chill in the refrigerator until thoroughly chilled.

3. Just before serving, whip the whipping cream with the remaining 2 tablespoons of sugar in a large bowl until it holds soft peaks. Pour the chilled eggnog mixture into a large punch bowl. Gently fold the whipped cream into the eggnog mixture just until combined. Garnish with freshly grated nutmeg.

GINGER FIZZ

SERVES 1

ginger ale
fresh mint sprigs, plus
extra to garnish
fresh raspberries,
to garnish

1. Put 1¾ ounces of ginger ale
   into a blender, add a few mint
   sprigs, and blend together.

2. Strain into a chilled highball glass
   filled two-thirds of the way with
   ice and top with more ginger ale.

3. Garnish with raspberries
   and the mint sprig.

CRANBERRY PUNCH

SERVES 10

2½ cups cranberry juice
2½ cups orange juice
5 ounces water
½ teaspoon ground ginger
¼ teaspoon cinnamon
¼ teaspoon grated
   nutmeg
sugared cranberries,
   to garnish
sugared mint leaves,
   to garnish

1. Put the first six ingredients into a saucepan and bring to a boil. Reduce the heat to low and simmer for 5 minutes.

2. Remove from the heat and pour into a heatproof pitcher or bowl. Chill in the refrigerator.

3. Remove from the refrigerator, put ice into the serving glasses, pour in the punch, and garnish with sugared cranberries and mint leaves on toothpicks.

CHAMPAGNE PICK-ME-UP

SERVES 1

1¾ ounces brandy
¾ ounce orange juice
¾ ounce lemon juice
dash grenadine
chilled champagne

1. Put ice into a cocktail shaker.

2. Pour the brandy, orange juice, lemon juice, and grenadine over the ice and shake vigorously until well frosted.

3. Strain into a chilled wine glass and top with champagne.

APPLE FIZZ

SERVES 1

4 ounces sparkling hard
    cider or apple juice
¾ ounce apple brandy
juice of ½ lemon
1 tablespoon egg white
generous pinch sugar
slices of lemon and
    apple, to garnish

1. Shake the first five ingredients together over ice.

2. Pour immediately into a glass.

3. Garnish with a slice of lemon and apple.

BOURBON MILK PUNCH

SERVES 1

1¾ ounces bourbon
2½ ounces milk
dash vanilla extract
1 teaspoon honey
freshly grated nutmeg,
    to garnish

1. Put ice into a cocktail shaker.

2. Pour the bourbon, milk, and vanilla extract over the ice.

3. Add the honey and shake until well frosted.

4. Strain into a chilled glass. Sprinkle with the grated nutmeg.

SPARKLING SNOW

SERVES 1

1½ ounces gin
½ ounce lemon juice
1 teaspoon simple syrup
¼ teaspoon edible
   silver glitter
chilled champagne

1. Shake the gin, lemon juice, and simple syrup, and edible glitter over ice until well frosted.

2. Strain into a chilled flute. Top with chilled champagne.

CLASSIC RUM PUNCH

SERVES 1

¾ **ounce fresh lime juice**
1¼ **ounces simple syrup**
1¾ **ounces golden rum**
lime curl, to garnish

1. Shake the lime juice, simple syrup, and golden rum over ice until well frosted.

2. Strain into a chilled cocktail glass filled with ice. Garnish with a long lime curl.

CHAPTER FIVE

Santa's coming to town...and he's been BUSY. And he may be a little tired. These cocktails are a perfect blend of flavors from Santa's favorite treats—maybe some that have been left out for him to sample—and feature some much-needed espresso or coffee to keep him wide awake on his travels.

SANTA'S DIMPLES

SERVES 1

½ ounce whiskey
½ ounce apple juice
splash green Chartreuse
club soda
mint sprig, to garnish

1. Stir the first three ingredients over ice, and strain into an ice-filled highball glass.

2. Top with club soda and garnish with a sprig of mint.

ESPRESSO GALLIANO

SERVES 1

1¾ ounces Galliano
sugar
freshly made strong
    black coffee
splash orange or
    lemon juice
orange zest strip,
    to garnish

1. Put the Galliano into a warmed heatproof glass and add sugar to taste.

2. Pour in the coffee and orange juice, and stir until the sugar has completely dissolved.

3. Garnish with the orange zest.

RUM ESPRESSO WITH WHIPPED CREAM

SERVES 4

⅔ cup heavy cream
1¼ cups hot espresso
   coffee
1 tablespoon rum
2 teaspoons raw
   sugar, plus extra
   for sprinkling

1. Pour the heavy cream into a bowl and whip until it holds soft peaks.

2. Mix the coffee, rum, and sugar in a liquid measuring cup and pour into four small heatproof glasses or coffee cups.

3. Gently drop spoonfuls of the cream into the coffee. Garnish with a sprinkle of additional sugar.

THE GRINCH

SERVES 1

1½ ounces midori liqueur
1 ounce white rum
5 ounces lemon lime
soda (or lemon
lime club soda)
maraschino cherry,
to garnish

1. Fill a glass with ice, then add midori liqueur and rum. Top with lemon lime soda and stir to combine.

2. Garnish with a maraschino cherry.

THE MRS. CLAUS

SERVES 1

1 cup eggnog
1½ ounces white
    chocolate liqueur
1 tablespoon peppermint
    schnapps
whole and crushed candy
    canes, to garnish

1. To garnish with the candy cane, add the water to a saucer, then crushed candy cane to a second saucer. Dip the rim of a glass first in the water, then in the candy.

2. Add the eggnog, white chocolate liqueur, and peppermint schnapps into a cocktail glass and stir to combine.

3. Garnish with a whole candy cane.

SANTA'S HEAD ELF

SERVES 1

1¼ ounces Irish whiskey
¾ ounce green curaçao
dry ginger ale
lime slice, to garnish

1. Stir the whiskey and curaçao in a glass with ice.

2. Top with ginger ale. Garnish with a slice of lime.

CRANBERRY ENERGIZER

SERVES 4

10 ounces (1¼ cups)
   cranberry juice
4 ounces champagne
4 ounces orange juice
½ cup fresh raspberries
½ ounce lemon juice
fresh orange slices,
   to garnish

1. Pour the cranberry juice, champagne, and orange juice into a blender and blend gently until combined.

2. Add the raspberries and lemon juice and blend until smooth.

3. Strain into glasses and garnish with the orange slices.

NOTE

For an nonalcoholic version of this cool drink, simply omit the champagne.

CHAPTER SIX

Whether you like cinnamon French toast or breakfast casserole, this collection of cocktails provides the perfect accompaniments to your Christmas brunch foods. And seasonal twists on drinks like the mimosa and the bloody mary add to the festivity.

MIMOSA

SERVES 1

1 passion fruit
½ ounce orange curaçao
chilled champagne
star fruit slice, to garnish

1. Put ice into a cocktail shaker.

2. Scoop out the passion fruit flesh into the shaker. Add the curaçao and shake until frosted.

3. Strain into a chilled champagne flute, top with champagne, and garnish with the star fruit slice.

CRANBERRY ORANGE CRUSH

SERVES 1

juice of 2 blood oranges
5 ounces cranberry juice
1 ounce raspberry (or
other fruit) syrup
sugar, to taste
chilled champagne
or prosecco

1. Shake the first four ingredients in a cocktail shaker until really frothy.

2. Pour straight into a cocktail glass and top with champagne or prosecco.

BRUNCH COBBLER COCKTAIL

SERVES 1

1 teaspoon granulated
   sugar
2 ounces sparkling water
3 ounces ruby port
orange slice and cocktail
   cherry, to garnish

1. Put the sugar into a chilled wine glass and add the sparkling water. Stir until the sugar has dissolved.

2. Fill the glass with ice and pour in the ruby port. Garnish with the orange slice and cocktail cherry.

RUDOLPH'S NOSE

SERVES 2

12 raspberries
½ ounce cream
¾ ounce framboise or
    raspberry syrup
chilled champagne

1. Set aside 2 unbruised raspberries.
   Blend the remainder with the
   cream, framboise, and crushed ice
   in a blender until frosted and slushy.

2. Pour into chilled glasses
   and top with champagne.
   Float a raspberry on top.

ORANGE AND GINGER ALE COCKTAIL

SERVES 1

1¾ ounces gin
¾ ounce fresh
    orange juice
ginger ale, to taste
orange slice, to garnish

1. Stir the gin and orange juice over ice in a medium tumbler.

2. Top with ginger ale and garnish with an orange slice.

BERRY BERRY RED

SERVES 1

½ cup raspberries
4 ounces raspberry juice
4 ounces cranberry juice
sparkling wine
1 small meringue,
    crumbled

1. Set aside 4 raspberries. In a blender, blend the remaining fruit with the juices and crushed ice.

2. Add the fruit slush to a chilled glass and top with sparkling wine.

3. Garnish with the reserved raspberries and the crumbled meringue.

SANTA'S SANGRIA

SERVES 10

1 (750ml) bottle of
   red wine
10 ounces orange juice
2½ ounces cranberry juice
2 ounces lemon juice
2 ounces lime juice
3½ ounces simple syrup
lemon, orange, and lime
   slices, to garnish

1. Put the wine, juices, and simple syrup into a chilled punch bowl and stir well.

2. Add ice and garnish with the slices of lemon, orange, and lime.

SILVER BERRY

SERVES 1

¾ ounce raspberry
  vodka, iced
¾ ounce crème de
  cassis. iced
¾ ounce Cointreau, iced
frozen raspberry,
  to garnish

1. Carefully and slowly layer
   the three liquors in the order
   listed, in a well-iced shot glass
   or tall thin cocktail glass.

2. They must be well iced first and may
   need time to settle into their layers.

3. Garnish with a frozen raspberry.

MERRY BLOODY MARY

SERVES 1

dash hot pepper sauce
dash Worcestershire sauce
1¾ ounces vodka
5¼ ounces tomato juice
juice of ½ lemon
pinch celery salt
pinch cayenne pepper
celery stalk and lemon
   slice, to garnish

1. Put ice into a cocktail shaker. Dash the hot pepper sauce and Worcestershire sauce over the ice.

2. Add the vodka, tomato juice, and lemon juice, then shake vigorously until well frosted.

3. Strain into a tall, chilled glass, add the celery salt and cayenne pepper, and garnish with the celery stalk and lemon slice.

COFFEE & CINNAMON EGGNOG

SERVES 4

4 ounces rum
2 cups milk
⅔ cup strong black coffee
1 cinnamon stick
2 extra-large eggs
⅓ cup granulated sugar
½ cup heavy cream
2 teaspoons ground
   cinnamon

1. Put the rum, milk, coffee, and cinnamon stick into a saucepan and heat over medium heat until almost boiling. Cool for 5 minutes, then remove and discard the cinnamon stick.

2. Put the eggs and sugar into a bowl and beat until pale and thick. Gradually beat in the rum, milk, and coffee mixture. Return to the pan and heat gently, stirring all the time, until just thickened. Cool for 30 minutes.

3. Put the cream into a bowl and whip until it holds soft peaks. Gently fold the cream into the egg mixture. Divide among four glasses, sprinkle with ground cinnamon. Serve immediately or chill for 1–2 hours in the refrigerator before serving.

CHAPTER SEVEN

IT'S A MARSHMALLOW WORLD

Make sure you have a cocktail nearby after you slide another holiday cookie sheet into the oven! The cocktails in this chapter feature ingredients from some of your favorite holiday bakes—and the addition of a little liqueur gives these innocent-tasting drinks a kick.

DRUNKEN SNOWMAN

SERVES 8

1 pint vanilla ice cream
16 ounces hot chocolate
4 ounces Irish
    cream liqueur
whipped cream, to serve
chocolate shavings,
    to garnish

1. Add two scoops of ice cream into each mug. Pour pour equal amounts of the hot chocolate and Irish cream liqueur on top.

2. Top with whipped cream and garnish with chocolate shavings.

GINGERBREAD MARTINI

SERVES 1

1½ ounces vodka
½ ounce hazelnut liqueur
2 ounces Irish
    cream liqueur
2 ounces gingerbread
    syrup
2 ounces heavy cream
    or half and half
crushed gingerbread
    cookies, to garnish

GINGERBREAD SYRUP
1 cup sugar
½ cup water
2 teaspoons ground
    ginger
1 teaspoon molasses
1 teaspoon ground
    cinnamon

1. Make the syrup: In a small saucepan, whisk together water, sugar, ginger, and cinnamon until sugar dissolves. Bring to a boil, stirring occasionally. Remove from heat, add molasses, and let steep for 10 minutes. Transfer to a heatproof container for storage.

2. Place crushed gingerbread cookies on a small plate or saucer. Wet the outside rim of a martini or coupe glass with water. Holding the glass by the stem, rotate the rim to coat with cookie crumbs.

3. Add the first five ingredients to a cocktail shaker with ice. Shake until well combined. Strain into the martini or coupe glass.

CANDY CANE COCKTAIL

SERVES 1

2 ounces strawberry
    vodka
4 dashes white crème
    de menthe
2½ ounces cranberry juice
1 candy cane, crushed,
    to garnish

1. Place crushed candy canes on a small plate or saucer. Wet the outside rim of a chilled martini glass with water. Holding the glass by the stem, rotate the rim to coat with candy.

2. In a cocktail shaker, combine vodka, crème de menthe, and cranberry juice with ice and shake until well combined. Strain into martini glass.

WINTER SNOWFLAKE

SERVES 1

1 tablespoon white
    chocolate chips
1 tablespoon caramel
    sauce
1 teaspoon vanilla extract
4 ounces milk
2 ounces Irish
    cream liqueur
whipped cream, to serve
ground cinnamon,
    to garnish

1. Add the white chocolate, caramel, vanilla, milk, and Irish cream liqueur to a small saucepan. Heat over medium-low heat, stirring frequently, until chocolate has melted and all ingredients have combined.

2. Remove from heat and pour into heatproof glass. Top with whipped cream, and garnish with a sprinkle of ground cinnamon.

CHOCOLATE MARTINI

SERVES 1

1¾ ounces vodka
¼ ounce crème de cacao
2 dashes orange
    flower water
orange peel twist,
    to garnish

1. Shake the vodka, crème de cacao, and orange flower water over ice until really well frosted.

2. Strain into the cocktail glass and garnish with a twist of orange peel.

THE BLIZZARD

SERVES 1

2¼ ounces bourbon
1½ ounces unsweetened
　cranberry juice
½ ounce lemon juice,
　freshly squeezed
1 ounce simple syrup
rosemary sprig, to garnish
cranberries, to garnish

1. Fill a cocktail shaker with ice, then pour in the bourbon, cranberry juice, freshly squeezed lemon juice, and simple syrup. Shake vigorously.

2. Place ice in a rocks glass. Strain the drink over the ice and garnish with a rosemary sprig and cranberries.

TANNENBAUM

SERVES 1

¾ ounce white crème
de cacao

¾ ounce green crème
de menthe

1. Put the ice in a cocktail shaker
   and pour in the crème de cacao
   and crème de menthe.

2. Shake vigorously for 10–20 seconds,
   until the outside of the shaker is
   misted. Strain into a shot glass.

ALMONDINE

SERVES 1

2½ ounces rum
1¾ ounces peach juice
4 ounces cold milk
few dashes almond
    extract
1–2 tablespoons honey
1 medium egg
toasted almonds,
    to garnish

1. Shake the ingredients together
    in a cocktail shaker with
    ice until well frosted.

2. Pour into a large cocktail
    glass or wine glass and
    garnish with almonds.

APPLE PIE CREAM

SERVES 1

4–6 ice cubes
3½ ounces hard
    apple cider
1 small scoop vanilla
    ice cream
club soda
cinnamon sugar and
    apple, to garnish

1. Put the ice into a blender and add the apple cider and ice cream.

2. Blend for 10–15 seconds, until frothy and frosted. Pour into a glass and top with club soda.

3. Garnish with a sprinkle of cinnamon sugar and an apple slice.

NOTE

For an nonalcoholic version of this sweet treat, use apple juice instead of the hard apple cider.

SPIKED HOT CHOCOLATE

SERVES 4-6

3 cups milk
1 cup heavy cream
½ cup sugar
¼ cup unsweetened
    cocoa powder
kosher salt
6 ounces milk chocolate,
    chopped
4 ounces alcohol of
    choice (bourbon, rum,
    Irish cream liqueur,
    coffee liqueur, etc.)
1 teaspoon pure
    vanilla extract
marshmallows and cocoa
    powder, to garnish

1. Combine the milk, heavy cream, sugar, cocoa powder, and a pinch of salt in a saucepan. Cook over medium heat, stirring occasionally, until the sugar and cocoa powder dissolve and the milk is steaming. Be careful not to bring to a boil.

2. Whisk in half of the chopped chocolate until melted, then whisk in the remaining chocolate until combined.

3. Remove from the heat and whisk in the vanilla and your alcohol of choice. Pour into mugs and garnish with marshmallows and a dusting of cocoa powder.

NOTE

Learn to make your own homemade marshmallows on page 188!

CHAPTER EIGHT

SILENT NIGHT

As busy days wind down and the empty dinner plates are stacked high, make yourself an after dinner drink that's sure to help you unwind and relax—especially if decaf coffee is used. Apart from tasting delicious, these cocktails will fill your home with warm and inviting aromas.

CINNAMON MOCHA

SERVES 6

8 ounces milk chocolate,
   broken into pieces
¾ cup light cream
4 cups freshly
   brewed coffee
5 ounces coffee liqueur
1 teaspoon ground
   cinnamon, plus
   extra to garnish
whipped cream,
   to garnish
chocolate shavings,
   to garnish

1. Put the chocolate in a large, heatproof bowl set over a saucepan of gently simmering water. Add the light cream and stir until the chocolate has melted and the mixture is smooth.

2. Pour in the coffee and coffee liqueur, add the cinnamon, and beat until foamy. If serving hot, pour into six heatproof glasses or mugs, top with whipped cream, a sprinkling of cinnamon, and the chocolate curls. If serving cold, remove the bowl from the heat and allow to cool, then chill in the refrigerator until required. Pour into six glasses or mugs, top with whipped cream, a sprinkling of cinnamon, and the chocolate shavings.

GOLD COFFEE

SERVES 1

¾ ounce dark rum
¾ ounce orange curaçao
2½ ounces strong,
    cold black coffee
1 scoop vanilla ice cream
2 teaspoons strained
    passion fruit juice

1. Put the dark rum, curaçao, and coffee into a blender with ice. Add some ice cubes and blend until slushy.

2. Pour into a chilled glass, add the ice cream, and spoon over the passion fruit juice.

CHRISTMAS COFFEE COCKTAIL

SERVES 1

¾ ounce Irish cream liqueur

¾ ounce almond liqueur

¾ ounce coffee liqueur

¾ ounce light cream

1. Pour the liqueurs and cream into a cocktail shaker filled with ice.

2. Shake well and strain into a chilled old-fashioned glass filled with ice cubes.

MOCHA CREAM

SERVES 2

7 ounces milk
2 ounces light cream
1 tablespoon brown sugar
2 tablespoons
    unsweetened
    cocoa powder
½ ounce coffee syrup or
    instant coffee powder
1¾ ounces alcohol of
    choice (bourbon, rum,
    Irish cream liqueur,
    coffee liqueur, etc.)
6 ice cubes
whipped cream and
    grated chocolate,
    to garnish

1. Put the milk, cream, and sugar into a food processor or blender and process until combined.

2. Add the cocoa powder, coffee syrup, and alcohol of choice. Process well, then add the ice cubes and process until smooth.

3. Pour the mixture into glasses. Garnish with whipped cream and a sprinkle of grated chocolate.

AMARETTO
COFFEE

SERVES 1

1¼ ounces amaretto
sugar
freshly made strong
    black coffee
½–1 ounce heavy cream

1. Put the amaretto into a
   warm heatproof glass and
   add sugar to taste.

2. Pour in the coffee and stir.

3. When the sugar has completely
   dissolved, pour in the cream slowly
   over the back of a spoon so that
   it floats on top. Don't stir—drink
   the coffee through the cream.

MRS. CLAUS'S AFTER DINNER DRINK

SERVES 1

½ ounce peppermint
  schnapps, chilled
¾ ounce Kahlúa, chilled
½ ounce Irish cream
  liqueur

1. Pour the peppermint schnapps into a chilled small wine glass.

2. Carefully pour the Kahlúa over the back of a spoon to make a second layer.

3. Finally, float the Irish cream liqueur on top.

MIDNIGHT'S KISS

SERVES 1

sugar
lemon wedge
½ ounce vodka
2 teaspoons blue curaçao
sparkling wine

1. Spread the sugar on a plate. Run a wedge of lemon around the rim of a chilled champagne flute to moisten it, then dip the glass in the sugar.

2. Add the vodka and curaçao to a shaker filled with ice.

3. Shake well, strain into the glass, and top with sparkling wine.

NOTE

You can use any sugar around the rim of the glass—or buy gold sugar from a specialty supplier to increase the glamour factor of this cocktail.

CHAPTER NINE

NOW BRING US SOME FIGGY PUDDING

While you won't find a recipe for figgy pudding in this chapter, you will find some festive and delicious recipes that pair well with the cocktails included in this book. From appetizers to brunch food to seasonal snacks and traditional cookies, there's bound to be something for everyone to enjoy with their holiday drink of choice.

OVERNIGHT CINNAMON ROLLS

Makes: 12 rolls | Prep: 30 mins | Bake: 30 mins

Nothing beats the smell of cinnamon rolls on Christmas morning. Enjoy these with a mimosa (page 119) or a Merry Bloody Mary (page 135).

DOUGH
½ cup granulated sugar
½ cup butter, melted
1 teaspoon salt
2 eggs
4 cups all-purpose flour
2 packets instant yeast
1 cup warm milk

FILLING
½ cup butter, softened
½ cup granulated sugar
½ cup brown sugar
1–2 tablespoons cinnamon

FROSTING
4 ounces cream cheese, softened
4 tablespoons butter, softened
1 teaspoon vanilla extract
2–3 tablespoons milk
2 cups confectioner's sugar
¼ teaspoon salt

1. Mix butter, sugar, and salt in a large bowl until combined. Then add the eggs and mix. Add in flour and instant yeast and stir to combine. Finally add in milk and mix until a soft, smooth dough forms.

2. On lightly floured surface, knead about 10-12 times, then place into a large well-oiled bowl. Cover and let dough rise for at least 30 minutes or until it's doubled in size.

3. Once risen, punch down dough and let rest for 5 minutes. Roll into a 14x8-inch rectangle on a lightly floured surface, then brush with softened butter.

4. In a bowl, combine granulated sugar, brown sugar, and cinnamon. Sprinkle over the buttered dough. Roll the dough into a log starting from the long side, then cut into 12 cinnamon rolls.

5. Place the cinnamon rolls in a 13x9-inch pan that has been brushed with butter. Cover the rolls with plastic wrap or foil and place rolls in the fridge to bake the following morning.

6. The next morning, remove from the fridge 30-60 minutes prior to your desired bake time. Let them rest in a warm place while the oven preheats to 350°F. Once the oven is heated, bake rolls for approximately 25–30 minutes or until lightly browned.

7. To make the frosting, stir together softened cream cheese and softened butter. Add in vanilla, salt, and milk and mix until combined. Add in confectioner's sugar and mix until smooth. If you would like thicker frosting, add more confectioner's sugar one tablespoon at a time. If you would like a thinner frosting, add more milk one teaspoon at a time until desired consistency is reached.

8. Once rolls are removed from oven, you can frost immediately or allow to cool slightly, then frost. Store any leftover rolls in the refrigerator.

BRUNCH CASSEROLE

SERVES 12 | PREP: 20 MINS
PLUS COOLING | BAKE: 30 MINS

Balance the savory flavors in this casserole with a sweet drink like a
Rudolph's Nose (page 124) or a Berry Berry Red (page 128).

4 cups frozen shredded
    hash browns, thawed
1 pound pork sausage,
    cooked and drained
½ pound bacon strips,
    cooked and crumbled
1 medium green bell
    pepper, chopped
1 green onion, chopped
2 cups shredded cheddar
    cheese, divided
4 large eggs
3 cups milk
1 cup biscuit baking mix
½ teaspoon salt

1. In a large bowl, combine the first five ingredients, then stir in 1 cup of cheese. Add to a greased 9x13-inch baking dish.

2. In another bowl, whisk eggs, milk, biscuit mix, and salt until blended, then pour over the ingredients in the baking dish. Sprinkle with the remaining cheese. Cover the baking dish with aluminum foil and refrigerate overnight.

3. When ready to eat, preheat oven to 375°F. Remove casserole from the refrigerator while the oven heats. Bake, uncovered, for 30–35 minutes or until a knife inserted into the center comes out clean. Let stand 10 minutes before cutting and serving.

CRANBERRY BRIE BITES

MAKES 24 | PREP: 20 MINS | BAKE: 15 MINS

These small bites are full of flavor and are even better paired with a glass of Jingle Juice Punch (page 82) or an Orange Cranberry Crush (page 120).

1 (8 ounces) tube crescent
   or puff pastry dough
cooking spray, for pan
flour, for surface
1 (8 ounces) wheel of brie
½ cup cranberry sauce
¼ cup pecans, chopped,
   optional
6 sprigs of rosemary,
   cut into 1-inch
   pieces, to garnish

1. Preheat oven to 375°F.

2. Grease a mini muffin tin with cooking spray. On a lightly floured surface, roll out crescent dough, then pinch together seams. Cut into 24 squares. Place squares into muffin tin molds.

3. Cut brie into small pieces and place on top of the crescent dough. Then add a spoonful of cranberry sauce, chopped pecans, if desired, and one sprig of rosemary.

4. Bake for about 15 minutes or until the crescent pastry is golden.

GINGERBREAD COOKIES

MAKES: ABOUT 30 | PREP: 20 MINS, PLUS CHILLING AND COOLING | BAKE: 9–10 MINS

Pair a few of these spiced cookies with cocktails like Coffee & Cinnamon Eggnog (page 136) and, of course, a Gingerbread Martini (page 143).

¾ cup unsalted butter, softened

¾ cup packed dark brown sugar

½ cup molasses

1 egg

1½ teaspoons vanilla extract

3½ cups all-purpose flour

¾ teaspoon baking soda

½ teaspoon salt

1 tablespoon ground ginger

1 tablespoon ground cinnamon

½ teaspoon ground allspice

½ teaspoon ground cloves

1. In a large bowl, beat the butter and brown sugar until completely smooth and creamy.

2. Add the molasses and beat on medium-high speed until combined, then beat in the egg and vanilla on high speed for 2 minutes.

3. In a separate bowl, whisk together the flour, baking soda, salt, ginger, cinnamon, allspice, and cloves.

4. On low speed, slowly mix the dry ingredients into the wet ingredients until combined.

5. Divide dough in half. Roll each half into ¼-inch thick discs between parchment paper. Chill discs for at least 3 hours or up to 3 days.

6. Preheat oven to 350°F. Line a baking sheet with parchment paper or silicone baking mats.

7. Remove one disc of chilled cookie dough from the refrigerator. Cut into shapes with cutters. Place shapes 1 inch apart on prepared baking sheets. Reroll dough scraps until all the dough is shaped. Repeat with remaining disc of dough.

8. Bake cookies for about 9–10 minutes, or until cookies are set in the middle and just starting to darken around the edges.

9. Allow cookies to cool for 5 minutes on the cookie sheet. Transfer to cooling rack to cool completely. Once completely cool, decorate as desired.

SUGAR COOKIES

MAKES ABOUT 4 DOZEN | PREP: 20 MINUTES BAKE: 10 MINUTES

These cookies are perfect left out for Santa on Christmas Eve. Even better if they're left with a Rum Espresso (page 107) or The Mrs. Claus (page 110).

3 cups all-purpose flour
1½ teaspoons baking powder
1 teaspoon fine sea salt
3 sticks unsalted butter, softened
2½ cups granulated sugar,
   plus extra for rolling
2 large eggs
1 tablespoon pure vanilla extract

1. Preheat the oven to 375°F. Line several baking sheets with parchment paper.

2. Mix the flour, baking powder, and salt in a medium bowl.

3. In a separate bowl, cream together the butter and sugar on high until light and fluffy. Next, turn the mixer on low and add the eggs and vanilla extract. Once combined, scrape the sides of the bowl.

4. With the mixer running on low, slowly add the flour mixture until fully combined.

5. Pour some sugar into another small bowl to coat the cookies. Scoop the dough out and roll into 1-inch balls. The dough will be soft and delicate—be careful to not overwork it. Roll each ball in the bowl to coat with sugar, then place each ball two inches apart on the baking sheets. Use the bottom of a drinking glass to press down on each ball, until it's ⅓– to ½-inch thick.

6. Bake for 9–11 minutes or until the edges are slightly golden and the centers have just barely set. Let the cookies completely cool before enjoying—or decorating!

CHOCOLATE CHUNK STIRRERS

MAKES 10-15 | PREP: 5-10 MINS, PLUS COOLING | COOK: 5-10 MINS

These stirrers add a bit more decadence to festive warm cocktails. Try adding one to a Brandy Hot Chocolate (page 61) or a Christmas Cow (page 77).

7 ounces semisweet chocolate, milk chocolate, or white chocolate, or a mixture, finely chopped

OPTIONAL TOPPINGS
2–4 tablespoons shredded coconut
2–4 tablespoons toasted nuts, chopped
2–4 tablespoons mini marshmallows
2–4 tablespoons chocolate sprinkles

1. Put the chocolate into a heatproof bowl set over a saucepan of gently simmering water and heat until melted. If using different chocolates, melt them in separate bowls, and mix to combine once melted.

2. Spoon the chocolate equally into each cup in a silicone mini cupcake or ice cube tray. Leave to cool slightly until the chocolate begins to thicken, then push a small wooden spoon, craft stick, or coffee stirrer into each cup so it stands upright.

3. While the chocolate is still soft, scatter each with the toppings of your choice, then leave to set.

4. To enjoy, stir one stick into a warm cocktail of choice until melted.

JINGLE POPCORN MIX

MAKES 8 (1-CUP) SERVINGS
PREP: 15 MINUTES PLUS COOLING

*Share a big bowl of this festive mix with friends along with a big batch cocktail,
like Santa's Sangria (page 131) or Christmas Punch (page 81).*

8 cups popped popcorn
2 ounces white baking
   chocolate, chopped
1 teaspoon butter
⅓ cup dried cranberries
¼ cup chopped walnuts
   (or nuts of choice)
¾ teaspoon salt

1. After making the popcorn, place it all in a large bowl. In the microwave, melt the white chocolate and butter in a microwave-safe bowl and stir until smooth. Pour over the popcorn and toss to coat. Next add the cranberries, nuts, and salt, and mix together.

2. Spread the mixture on wax paper to cool until the chocolate has set. Store in an airtight container.

HOMEMADE MARSHMALLOWS

MAKES ABOUT 30 MARSHMALLOWS
COOK: 25 MINUTES, PLUS RESTING TIME

These marshmallows add a luxurious element to warm drinks like the Salted Caramel Rum Hot Cocoa (page 65) or the Rum Noggin (page 74).

¾ cup water, divided
3 (.25 ounce) packages
   unflavored gelatin
⅔ cup light corn syrup
2 cups granulated sugar
1 tablespoon vanilla extract
¼ cup cornstarch
¼ cup confectioner's sugar

1. Line a 9x9-inch baking dish with plastic wrap and spray with non-stick cooking spray. Spray another piece of plastic wrap to cover the top. Set aside.

2. Place ½ cup of water in a bowl and sprinkle in gelatin to soak.

3. While gelatin is soaking, combine ¼ cup of water, corn syrup, and granulated sugar in a saucepan. Bring the mixture to a boil over medium heat. Boil the mixture for 1 minute.

4. Carefully pour the hot sugar mixture into the gelatin mixture and beat on high for twelve minutes with an electric mixer. Beat until the mixture is fluffy and forms stiff peaks. Then add in the vanilla extract and beat until combined.

5. Pour the mixture into the prepared baking dish and use a greased spatula to smooth the top. Cover the top with the piece of prepared plastic wrap, pressing it down lightly to seal the covering to the top of the marshmallow. Allow the marshmallow candy to rest for 4 hours or overnight.

6. In a shallow bowl, mix together the cornstarch and confectioner's sugar. Using greased scissors or a greased kitchen knife, cut the marshmallow candy into strips, then into 1-inch squares. Dredge the marshmallows lightly in the cornstarch mixture and store in an airtight container.

INDEX